1.4

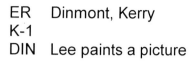

Lee
Paints a
Picture

A Book about Colors

BY KERRY DINMONT

Published by The Child's World®
1980 Lookout Drive • Mankato, MN 56003-1705
800-599-READ • www.childsworld.com

Photographs ©: Vadym Zaitsev/Shutterstock Images, cover, 1; ESB
Professional/Shutterstock Images, 3; Aleksandr Lupin/Shutterstock
Images, 4–5; Maxim Ibragimov/Shutterstock Images, 6; Keren Seg/
Shutterstock Images, 8–9; Rudchenko Lillia/Shutterstock Images, 10–11;
Igor Bondarenko/Hemera/Thinkstock, 12–13; iStockphoto, 14, 17;
Igor A. Bondarenko/Shutterstock Images, 18; Africa Studio/Shutterstock
Images, 20

Design Elements: Shutterstock Images

ISBN 9781503820135
LCCN 2016960936

Printed in the United States of America
PA02339

Today, Lee paints a picture.

What colors does

he use?

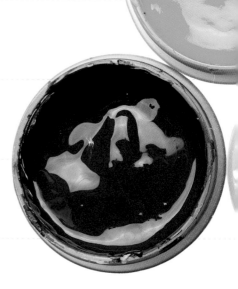

Lee paints in art class.

He has blue, yellow,

and red paint.

Lee learns that yellow, blue, and red are **primary colors**. They can **mix** to make other colors.

Lee paints his family.

He paints their pants

blue.

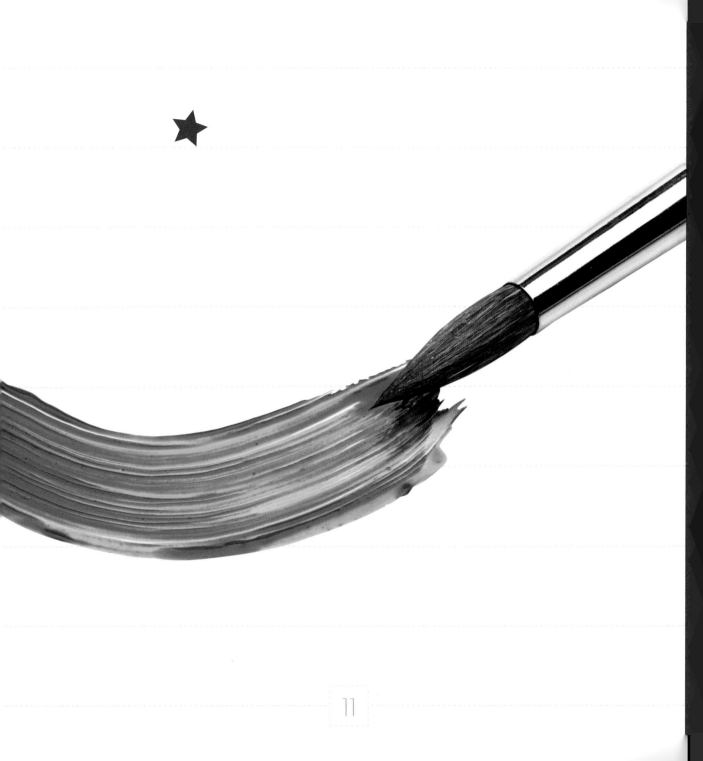

Lee uses red for Dad's shirt. The red and blue mix. Red and blue make purple.

13

Then some yellow
paint drips onto the
red paint. Lee **swirls**
his brush in the colors.

The color turns orange.
He uses this color for
his sister's shirt.

17

Next Lee mixes yellow and blue. It turns green! He paints his mom's shirt green.

What colors do you
like to paint with?

Words to Know

mix (MIKS) To mix is to combine different things. We mix yellow and blue to make green.

primary colors (PRY-mayr-ee KUHL-urz) The three primary colors are red, yellow, and blue. Primary colors can be mixed to make other colors.

swirls (SWURLZ) Something swirls when it is moved with a twisting motion. With his paintbrush, Lee swirls colors together.

Extended Learning Activities

1 Have you ever mixed colors? What colors were they? What colors did they make?

2 What color does red and blue make? What color does red and yellow make? What color does yellow and blue make?

3 What words in this story appeal to the sense of sight?

To Learn More

Books

Pantone Colors. New York, NY: Abrams Appleseed, 2012.

Schwake, Susan. *Art Lab for Kids: 52 Creative Adventures in Drawing, Painting, Printmaking, Paper, and Mixed Media—for Budding Artists of All Ages.* Beverly, MA: Quarry Books, 2012.

Tullet, Hervé. *Mix It Up!* San Francisco, CA: Handprint Books, 2014.

Web Sites

Visit our Web site for links about colors:
childsworld.com/links

Note to Parents, Teachers, and Librarians: We routinely verify our Web links to make sure they are safe and active sites. So encourage your readers to check them out!

About the Author

Kerry Dinmont is a children's book author who enjoys art and nature. She lives in Montana with her two Norwegian elkhounds.